74

917 E
Copy #1

A Week
in Leonora's World:
PUERTO RICO

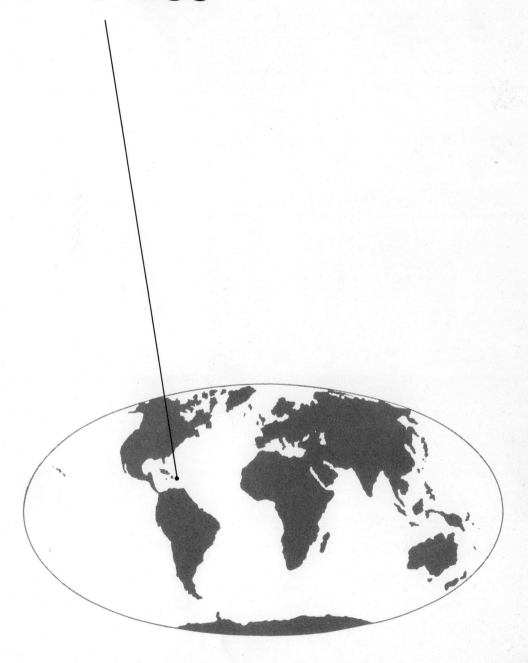

A Week in Leonora's World: PUERTO RICO

Photographs and text by Eliot Elisofon

Crowell-Collier Press, New York • Collier-Macmillan Limited, London

Library of Congress Catalog Card Number: 72-146610
The Macmillan Company, 866 Third Avenue, New York, New York 10022 • Collier-Macmillan Canada Ltd., Toronto, Ontario
Printed in the United States of America • 10   9   8   7   6   5   4   3   2   1

Leonora Figueroa is eight years old
and lives in San Juan, the capital
of Puerto Rico. This beautiful island
in the Caribbean Sea is part of the
United States, but once belonged to
Spain. This explains the Spanish names
San Juan, which means Saint John,
and Puerto Rico, which means Rich Port.

Leonora learns both English and Spanish
in school. She is a good student and
is often asked to read aloud. But,
like most children, she looks forward
to the play period between classes.

Leonora does her homework every day as soon as she comes home from school. Because the climate is so warm in Puerto Rico, she likes to kick off her shoes and go barefoot. The tiled floor feels cool beneath her toes.

Leonora has been studying the piano since she
was five years old. All her family is musical.
Her father, who often listens to her practice,
is a professional musician who plays the cello.
She plays her exercises so well that he gives
her a quarter for ice cream. After changing from
the play suit she wears at home to a favorite dress,
Leonora enjoys her treat in the small park nearby.

The next day, school lets out early and Leonora
has lunch at home. She is having soup, a piece
of fried chicken, cake, and milk for lunch.
But often in the Figueroa home, there are typical
Puerto Rican and Spanish dishes
like chicken cooked with seasonings and rice.

The market in San Juan sells vegetables and fruits that grow in the tropical climate of Puerto Rico. Leonora and her mother are shopping for plantains, a type of banana that must be cooked before it is eaten.

There are fewer than thirty
students in Leonora's class,
so her teacher has time
to work with each of them.

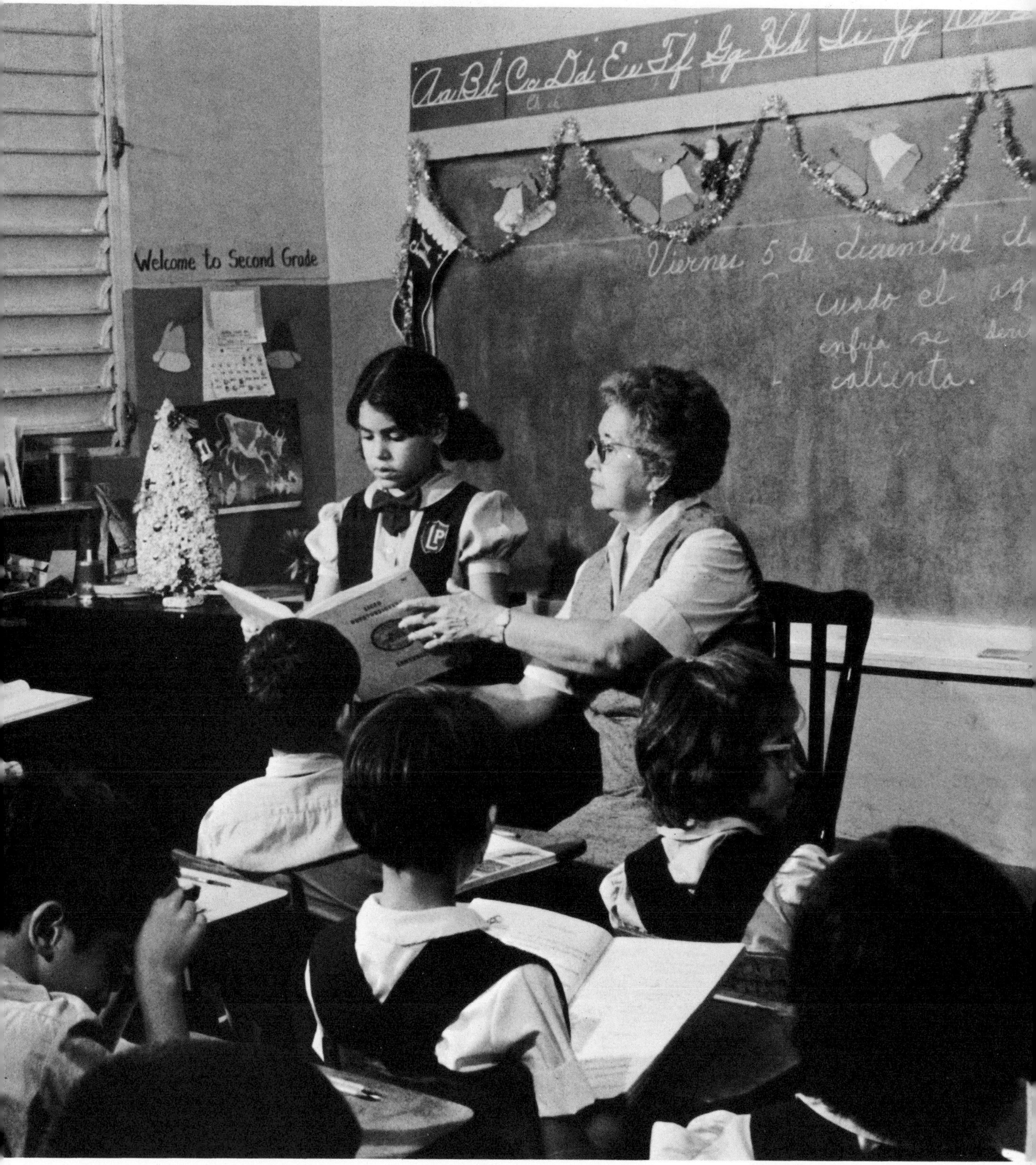
Welcome to Second Grade

Lunch period is fun after a hard arithmetic lesson,
especially when you can buy your lunch at the school canteen.

Leonora's best friend is Juanita. She is in the same class at school and lives on the same street. Riding their bicycles together, they pass by rows of Spanish-style houses with their many arches, balconies, and iron grills.

Leonora studies piano twice a week with one of her aunts.
A picture of Beethoven, one of the greatest composers
and pianists, stares down from the wall.
Something about his stern look makes Leonora want
to play her very best.

Later in the week, while Leonora and her
friends wait outside the school for their
mothers to pick them up, she reads them
a story in Spanish called "Pueblo y Campo."
This means "Town and Country."

The girls' uniforms are all the same, navy
blue jumpers with white blouses. The
boys wear blue shorts and white shirts. And
everybody wears blue socks and black shoes.

Families in Puerto Rico are close, and Leonora often plays with her cousins. One of them, Jaime, is old enough to supervise an outing. He calls to her outside her house on Saturday to join them in a ferry ride in San Juan harbor.

There are two flags flying on the ferry boat—the fifty stars and thirteen stripes of the United States and the five stripes and one star of Puerto Rico.

GUSTAVO BERGNES BERRIOS

Their ferry passes another one traveling in the opposite direction. Many people take the ferry not to go anywhere but just because it is such a pleasant ride.

Leonora and her cousins can see some of the buildings of
San Juan from the ferry, but if they were in an airplane...

...*this* is what San Juan would look like.

Hundreds of years ago, many countries fought
over the islands in the Caribbean. The Spaniards
built this fort, Morro Castle, on the shore near
San Juan, to protect the city from invasion by sea.
Leonora and her cousins visit the fort on Saturday
afternoon after the ferry ride.

The children are exploring the lowest part of the
fort near the sea. It is easy among these huge
stone walls to pretend that pirates are attacking
San Juan. Boom! You can almost
hear the cannons roar.

Leonora's cousins have an early dinner with her family that evening. The main dish is typically Puerto Rican—meat stewed with beans and other vegetables. After Leonora has helped with the dishes, she plays on the balcony with her cousin Jose and listens to her brother. He will not study piano or violin but prefers the guitar.

Leonora's father has four brothers, all professional musicians, and together they play as the Figueroa Quintet. They are well known in Puerto Rico and give many concerts there as well as in other countries of Latin America. On Saturday night they practice at the home of their father, Leonora's grandfather. Filled with pride in his sons, he sits apart wearing the Spanish cap called a *boina*. Leonora, too, loves to listen and is very quiet during the rehearsal.

The Figueroas enjoy the shore and spend many Sundays there.
One of the nice things about the beaches in Puerto Rico
is that you can swim all year round. Many American tourists
come there in the winter from cities like Chicago and
New York where it gets very cold. But the beach where
Leonora has gone with her mother and her cousins is rocky,
and there are no tourists there.

Music and dancing are very popular in Puerto Rico, so it is no surprise to Leonora to come upon some teenagers doing a *bomba* on the beach. This dance came to Puerto Rico from Africa. Leonora has learned in school that Puerto Ricans are descended from three important groups of people—Indian, African, and Spanish. Many Puerto Ricans are a mixture of all three.

There are lots of games to be
played on the beach. Hide-and-seek
is one of Leonora's favorites.
When the children are tired, they
settle down in a shady spot with
coconuts they have bought. How
cool and sweet the coconut "milk"
tastes after playing in the
tropical sun.

There are pretty shells along the edge of the sea,
but the tide is high and they are hard to find.
There are also sharp rocks under the water and
the sun is going down. Now it is time to go home.
Back to school tomorrow, thinks Leonora,
but it *was* a happy weekend.

DATE DUE
